"In *Weweni*, as the title suggests, Meg Noodin does indeed tread with care as she weaves a lyric vision of Anishinaabe experience—a twenty-first-century vision colored throughout with strands of our vibrant past and hopeful, if changed, future. Through poetry that attends both to an 'exhausted' world in which 'dried berries become rumors' and an 'undefeated' world inhabited by 'golden-feathered half-breeds,' this volume brings us into intimate connection with elements that animate our everyday: ice carvings, 'firm honor beats' at the drum, ceremonial sticks, 'sweet water sap of . . . dreams,' and fragile 'bones, smaller than sound.' Offered in two languages—Anishinaabemowin and English—on their journey to 'un-make war,' these poems sing stories filled with ancestors, offer advice for leadership and survival, but perhaps most importantly, paint us into a landscape lush with the implacable night sky and the creatures with whom we share this mythic earth— 'panting the same wind.'"

—Kimberly Blaeser, author of *Apprenticed to Justice*

"These are excellent poems in English and in Anishinaabemowin—they give us the bones of the language always backed up by the hush of the trees, the water, the beauty of the land where speaking arose to express our relatedness. This is a book of dreams and cautions that reaches out to the reader time and again with humor, quiet wonder, wit, joy, and companionship. Simply lovely."

—Heid E. Erdrich, author of *Cell Traffic*

"*Weweni* offers readers a stunning, crystalline collection of poems—full of wisdom, deep and calm, drawn from living languages reaching through time and space to bring us closer to the poetic wonder of living in language. A skilled artist's work shows here, creating awareness with the touch of word and sound, resonating syllable by syllable, with love of language, known to all of us who have imagined each part of the world, holding some immanent potential for poetic expression."

—Gordon Henry, enrolled member of the White Earth Chippewa Tribe of Minnesota and professor in creative writing and American Indian studies at Michigan State University

"Noodin's poems are the gifts life can be built on. They truly illustrate *weweni*, deep care and consideration, for all of who we have been, are, and will be as Anishinaabeg. These words—invested with a fierce love and commitment to our language and community—are a revolution. *Miigwech*, Margaret."

—Niigaanwewidam Sinclair, Department of Native Studies, University of Manitoba

Weweni

Made in Michigan Writers Series

Weweni

poems

in Anishinaabemowin

and English

by Margaret Noodin

Wayne State University Press
Detroit

19 18 17 16 15   5 4 3 2 1

ISBN 978-0-8143-4038-7 (paperback)
ISBN 978-0-8143-4039-4 (e-book)

Library of Congress Control Number: 2014946512

Publication of this book was made possible by
a generous gift from The Meijer Foundation.
Additional support was provided by Michigan Council for Arts
and Cultural Affairs and National Endowment for the Arts.

Designed and typeset by Bryce Schimanski
Composed in Adobe Garamond Pro

Wenji gidebwetawininim.

Contents

Preface

In his book, *The Space of Literature*, Maurice Blanchot wrote, "We rediscover poetry as a powerful universe of words where relations, configurations, forces are affirmed through sound, figure, rhythmic mobility, in a unified and sovereignly autonomous space. Thus the poet produces a work of pure language, and language in this work is its return to its essence" (42). The poems here are an attempt to reflect the essence of Anishinaabemowin. They were written first in Anishinaabemowin and then in English, which is why the Anishinaabemowin versions are more complex and musical. In many cases, the sounds and juxtapositions of meaning add layers of action and imagery. Because Anishinaabemowin is the focus of the collection, the English version of each poem is not always a literal translation and serves primarily as a lyric explanation.

Anishinaabemowin is the language of a group who refer to themselves as "the People of the Three Fires"—the Odawa, Potawatomi, and Ojibwe—who migrated from the eastern Atlantic area to the Great Lakes watershed thousands of years ago. According to oral history, it was the language used by Nanaboozhoo; according to written records, it was one of several languages used during the fur trade era from the seventeenth to the nineteenth century, with multinational speakers of Anishinaabemowin in Montreal, Detroit, Chicago, Duluth, and along the mighty Michiziibing. It is currently used in more than two hundred Anishinaabe communities in Quebec, Ontario, Manitoba, Saskatchewan, Alberta, North Dakota, Michigan, Wisconsin, and Minnesota.

As for the word itself, the Anishinaabe people could be called "the good people." *Nishin,* as a statement, means "good" or "excellent." The ending *mowin* is added to any ethnic designation to indicate the language of that group. Taking the word *Anishinaabemowin* apart a bit more, the *mow* means it is a verb of exchange between two—people, trees, ghosts, even apples or mittens, technically anything that a speaker classifies by habit or logic as animate. The *in* at the end turns the word into a noun. The middle of the word is a bit harder to define, and that is precisely as it should be. As with many indigenous languages, speakers delight in the fluid functionality of the lexicon. One never knows how words will be manipulated to create new meaning. Some see in *aabe* the word for "masculine," while others say it stems from the description of being lowered to earth. Perhaps both are right, perhaps in some ancient dialect both have yet another, now forgotten, meaning. Like all words, and like the language itself, Anishinaabemowin has a life of its own and is shaped by speakers who use it.

The spelling system used in this volume is called Fiero Double Vowel and was created by Charles Fiero, who worked with fluent speakers in the late 1950s. It is used by Anishinaabe teachers, elders, translators, administrators, language activists, and students seeking a common orthography. Although this system of writing is used in many communities, speakers also recognize the importance of syllabic alphabets and folk-phonetic systems. I chose to use the Fiero system because it is what I use with my own students, friends, and family. I've also carefully included many vowels, including those sometimes not pronounced, which reflects a more western dialect familiar to speakers in Minnesota and Wisconsin. The poems here may sound new and unusual, as a poet might argue they should, but most of the words can easily be recognized by Ojibwe speakers in Michigan and Ontario as well as by Odawa and Potawatomi speakers who use variations of Anishinaabemowin. Of course, there are spellings, pronunciations, and vocabulary choices that make the language of each community distinct, but it is important for readers and the next generation of speakers to know that in our similarities we find meaning, and in our differences we find opportunity.

The history of this volume extends back to the 1970s when I found, in Minneapolis, Minnesota, two small chapbooks of poems. Luckily it was Gerald Vizenor's *Summer in the Spring* I encountered first, where he demonstrated the sophisticated imagery of the Anishinaabe dream-song format. He spoke of the short poems as an editor, respectfully curating on the page a shared communal truth with a literary precedent and a critical future. He reintroduced to modern readers the shape and content of Anishinaabe verse as it was first presented to readers of English in 1886. His collection was based on a belief in continuance and the survival of indigenous languages. What I try to do now is carry this tradition into the future, allowing the Anishinaabe language to fully define the poems, rather than serve as a semiotic accent to predominantly English writing.

The reason we need more modern writing in indigenous languages is to avoid what I found in the other book, A. Poulin Jr.'s *Catawba: Omens, Prayers and Songs*. A fine poet and translator himself, Poulin "re-expressed" Catawba lyric verses in 1977 that had been spoken in 1934 by the last four individuals to grow up speaking only Catawba. Unfortunately, Poulin wrote, "the language is gone," which, he explained, "assumes an even more stark and brutal dimension that conjures an image of a nation without tongues, a communal spirit forever speechless, a people's exchange with creation forever silenced. It testifies to what extent the language of a people is as precious as it is fragile, utterly vulnerable to a kind of violence we still don't recognize or admit to." It is correct to acknowledge that with the passing of a generation, there is the risk of losing the creative genius of fluent ancestors. However, according to the Catawba Nation in 2013, "the Catawba language has been restored and is taught in our children's programs." So, perhaps it is not correct to announce the death knell of languages that, once sleeping, are surviving, evolving, and working their way toward new futures. Analysis will show modern children use ancestral indigenous language differently, less often, and in ways their elders might not even recognize, but if they are Catawba children, expressing their views without using English, they represent a continuity of "communal spirit." It is this communal spirit I attempt to continue in Anishinaabemowin.

Poulin described Catawba verse as "repetitious, awkward, staccato" and "alien." Vizenor described Anishinaabe verse as "descriptive," "euphonious," and "a sympathy of cosmic rhythms and tribal instincts." Clearly, perspectives on indigenous poetics vary greatly and readers need more opportunities to experience indigenous language and literary arts. In these Anishinaabemowin poems, readers will find more vowels, unusual consonant combinations, and repeated syllables that ripple through words. To sound out the vowels as they are written here, remember the following:

> A single *a* sounds like the *u* in *cup.*
> Double *aa*'s sound like the *a* in *father.*
> One *e* sounds like the *e* in the French word *café,* or sometimes like the *e* in *bet.*
> One *i* sounds like the *i* in words like *bit, little, sip.*
> Two *ii*'s sound like the *ee* or *ea* in *knee, peach or each.*
> A single *o* may sound like the *au* in *caught,* or the *u* in *put.*
> Double *oo*'s sound like the *o* in *boat, know,* or *toe.*

Consonants represent the same sounds as in English, but *f, l, r, v,* and *x* are never used. There are also consonant clusters, which give a different dimension of sound to the language. Be sure to say them slowly as you encounter them in words: *sk, shp, sht, shk, mb,* and *nd.*

The poems in this volume attempt to forge a chain of continuance in all directions—ancient, future, and across the difficult present where the language itself will either be lowered into our hearts and used through our days, or follow our elders' bones as they slowly become part of the bundle that is earth. It really is that stark, the edge on which we stand. Read on, read out loud, and wrestle the consonant clusters because that is what helps us all step away from the edge of forgetting.

Weweni

Bizindamaang

Noodin ninoondaan nanagoodinong
apii "ziiziigwaa" nagamowaad zhingwag
apii shkwandamag mawiiwaad
apii baapagishkaawaad waasechiganag.

Miidash gwekaanimad, boonaanimad nengatch piitaanimad.

Noongwa jiisakinini da shkitoon weweni jiisakaanke
miinawaa maajigaaskanozowaad noodinong.

Gekaajigba wiindamaaiyangidwa, "bimaadiziig ezhi-wiindeyeg."

Mikojiinaang debwemigad nikananang
giishpin bizindamaang.

Listening

I hear the wind sometimes
when the pines sing "ziiziigwaa"
when the doors cry
when the windows shake.

Then the wind shifts, lets up and slows to a new speed.

Now the tent shaker carefully builds his tent
and the wordless whispers begin.

The old ones tell us, "live as you are named."

We sense the truth in our bones
if we listen.

Gimbiiskaabiimin Apane

Apii mooshkine aapkizid
naawiying odo'shkiinzhig okomis
ani-waabamowin
zhooniyaabikwe mbikwaakwad
oshki-nookaazhe
giizhigong.

negweyab-aawanan babaamishimo
misko-miin-aazhe
miin-aazhe
bimide miinawaa bingwiin
oshki'anoongkewaad
oshki'aadisookewaad.

Dibikibagoneyaa temigad
bakaan bagodakamig
kina gojing
gaawiin ningoji
zaagigi, zaagakii
epichii bangishimod.

Gimbiiskaabiimin apii nagamoying
ginebigog, goon
mitigwaanan, miigwanag
nibwaakaaying abinoojiwiying
nibaaying waaboowaning
mashko'asabikeying.

We Are Returning Always

When the moon is full
the center of grandmother's eye
becomes a mirror,
a ball of silver hair,
the spot of new skin
in the sky.

The nebulae dance behind her
raspberry light
blueberry light
gas and dust
making new stars
and new stories.

A dark hole discerned
is a different wilderness
everywhere
and nowhere
growing, expanding
while collapsing.

And our song returns us
snakes and snow
twigs and twine
we are wise bright infants
asleep in a blanket
spun of energy.

Waabowayaan

Waabowayaanong soswaning

name mashtanishi-oningwiiganan

ninoshenhsag niimiwaad waabmagwa

nanagodinong zhikeyawaad

nanagodinong niizhiwaad

gibaako-waamjigaazowaad

saakonendamowaad

nookaa-zhoomingweniwaad miinawaa

mashkawiden.

Blankets

In a nest of blankets

beneath woolen wings

I can see my aunts dancing

sometimes alone

sometimes in pairs

eyes closed

minds open

smiles soft and

strong hearts.

Waawiindamojig

Nangodinong
niizhing gimewon
mii wi apii gii giiwanimowaad.

Akiwenziiyag biiminawag
bingwi-waawiindamaadiwinan
gii waawiindamaadiwaad enji-zaagiding.

Mindimooyensag gibozanaawaan
dibajimowinan biinish ombishkaa
awaasa debwetaagwag.

Nooshensag ozaagiaawaan
zaam gashkitoowaad
anishaa'endamowaad ezhi-maadiziwaad.

Oniijaanishag gii zegiziwag
zaam gikendamowaad ingoding
waa ezhi-dibaajimowaad.

The Promisers

Sometimes
the rain came twice
and that is when they lied.

The old men twisted
the dusty promises
they once made as young lovers.

The old ladies baked
the tales until they rose
beyond believability.

The grandchildren adored them
for this ability to
re-imagine their lives.

Their own children were frightened
by the idea of what they
would say themselves one day.

Okanan

Apii jiibay bi dagooshinod
okanan nandawaabandaanan
gii gaadooyaan baatiindoon
ishkweyaang ndo'dengwekaajigan.

Nisimdana-ashi-niswi beshabiiaag
manidoominensag inaabiiginaag
oningwiiganan gaawiin tesiinon
onzowan gaawiin tesiinon.

Niizhtana-ashi-niizhwaaswi nindayaanan
wii aabjitooyaan ji-ezhininjiishiyaan
maage giiwitaajiishinidiying ji-maamwizhibiiamaang
dibaajimowinan e-waamjigaadeg.

Miidash dibishkoo makwa
ningwayakogaabow
gichikaanan biiskamowaad
mashkawiziwinan ji-maajaayaan.

Okanensan agaasin apii enewewin
gibaakogaadeg nipigemagong
apii ziitaaganimiskwimamaangaashkaamagag
bimiwidoowaad kaakazhewaabik waabanong mii ningaabii'anong.

Gaawiin tesiinon okanan
niindibong apii bwaajigeyaan,
nin'dooning apii jiim'inan,
ndo'neseng apii mamigaadeg.

Gaawiin tesiinon okanan
apii oshkibimaadiziwinkeying,
debiziying apii zaagidiying,
mawigaazoying, anamaegaazoying,

Mii sa nindan niibina gego
gashkigaadooyaan
apii jiibay bi dagooshin
okanan nandawaabandaang.

Bones

When the ghost visits
looking for bones
I have some hidden
behind my mask.

I have a line of thirty-three
beads strung between
an absence of wings
to where there is no tail.

I have twenty-seven of them
I use to make one handprint
or curl together to write
stories that can be seen.

And when like a bear
I balance my height
the largest bones wear
ropes of strength in motion.

But the bones smaller than sound
are kept in a cage near my heart
where red saltwater waves
carry calcium east then west.

There are no bones
in my mind when I dream,
on my mouth when I kiss,
on my breath when it is taken away.

There are no bones
when we make new life,
fall in love satisfied,
cry or pretend to pray.

These are the things
I can hide
when the ghost visits
looking for bones.

Jaaganige

Gomaapii booch igo jaaginigewag.
Gaaski-wiiyaas giishkidon.
Baatemiinan babaamaadojigaade.
Gakina gego gii jaaginigaade.
Waawaashkeshag gii goziwag.
Opiichiwag aapchigo onanaandonaawaan
mooseg, manidoonsag miinawaa Gizhemanido.
Miinawaa ginanaandonaan ishkodens
ji-jaagaakizaman gaawiin ezhinikaadesiinoon.

Exhausted

After a while it is time to run out.
The dried meat cuts your mouth.
The dried berries become rumors.
Everything has been used.
The deer have moved camp.
The robins are dedicated to the search
for worms, insects, and a new God.
And you search for the matches
to set fire to the unnamed.

Bichibowin

Ogiigikendaan ina nitam-pogozid
ezhi-nandawaabandang
ezhi-maamiginang
dakwandang maagizhaa onzang
ojiibikan, inashkoon, niibiishan maagizhaa miinan?

Anish-minik ji-noojimod?
Anishi-minik ji-bichibod?

Gii baabinchiged ina ayaapii
anaamizaagiiaasiged
giiwenizhaawaad jiibayag
ishkwa bijipidaminid maaji-maashkiki?

Poison

How did the first taster know
where to search
when to gather
whether to bite or boil
roots, stems, leaves, or seeds?

How much would heal?
How much would poison?

Did she sometimes wait
in the summer heat
for the ghosts to send her back
after a taste of bad medicine?

Waagaatigoog

Anishinaabeg gii owaangawi'aawaan
weweni waagibizhaawaad
waawiyebii'igewaad
aadisookaanag biskitenamowaad
wiikwiiwin waabandamowaad
wiikongewaad ji-dibenindizowaad
enji-waatebagaa.

---

*Apii Anishinaabeg gaa waagaatigoog waabamaawaad, gikendamowaad
mino-nagishkodaadiwin. Gakina awiya gii bimaawadaasowag Anaamakamig
Biiwaabikomiikanan wiijikiwenimaawaad Odaawaag, Bodewaadamiig
miinawaa Ojibweg.*

Crooked Trees

The Anishinaabe tamed them
bending them carefully
making compasses
of stories folded
of energy visible
an invitation to freedom
in each spent leaf.

Crooked trees marked paths and safe meeting places across the Anishinaabe nation. For this reason, those who travelled the Underground Railroad found friends among the Odawa, Potawatomi, and Ojibwe people.

Nayendamowin Mitigwaaking

Apii dibikong gaashkendamoyaan miinawaa goshkoziyaan
endogwen waa ezhichigewaad bagwaji Anishinaabensag odenang,
mitigwaaking izhaayaan miinawaa anweshimoyaan.

Nimawadishaag zhingwaakwag miinawaa okikaandagoog.
Nimbizindawaag zhashagiwag miinawaa ajiijaakwag.
Niwiiji-ayaawaag zaagaa'iganing ogaawag miinawaa apakweshkwayag.
Nimaamakaadendaanan miikanan miinawaa asabikeshiwasabiig.

Apii biidaaban miidash niswi giiwosewag miinawaa
niizhwaaswi nimiseyag bwaawaabanjigaazowaad
baabimoseyaan nikeyaa naawakweng zoongide'eyaan.

Woodland Liberty

When in the night I am weary and wondering
what the wild young Anishinaabeg of the cities will do,
I go into the woods and rest.

I visit with the white pines and the jack pines.
I listen to the herons and the cranes.
I share the lake waters with the walleye and the cattails.
I marvel at the complexity of wild paths and webs woven.

Then when the dawn hides the three hunters
and seven sisters of the night sky
I walk bravely toward the noonday.

Ozhaawaashkaazo

Naambiig jibwaa minokaming
Mishibizhiw aandaawe.
Apii giizis zaagiaasige
giiskang ozhaawaashkwaande babiinzikawaagan
biiskang ozhaawaashkwaande
nitaa-niimid nitaagibiiwazod
ashaamaad, ashaamaad
giizhigag, dibikag
zaagiiaasi-miijimke
migoshkaaji'aad akiinan
baashkaabigwaniid.

Blue-Green Becoming

Under the shore before Spring
the Water Panther changes colors
taking off his blue coat
putting on his green coat
dancing brilliantly covered in algae
feeding, feeding
the days and nights
making food of sunshine
teasing earth to bloom.

Dibiki-Ziigwaagaame

Ziigwaagame nindondaa'aagominaan
makademashkikiwaaboo miinawaa
gagwejimadizod, "Aniin e-naagamin
dibikiziigwaagame?"

Gete-biwaabikokaadakik ina?
Giizhik ina?
Zagaswans ina?

maagizhaa

Oningwiigan aandeg ina?
Moozo ozaawaabi ina?
Oshki miikanens mitigwakiing ina?
Ode noondan abita-dibikong ina?

miidash nisidotamaan

Wiishkobii-makade-aagamide
bimaadiziwin e-naagamin.

Question: Why is some maple syrup is dark and some is light?
Answer: Because some we boil at night.

Jim Northrup in Walking the Rez Road

Night Syrup

I stir sweet maple into coffee
And I ask myself,
"What is the flavor
of night syrup?"

An ancient iron kettle?
Northern cedar?
A lick of smoke?

or

The wing of a crow?
The brown eye of a moose?
A new path in the woods?
The sound of a heartbeat at midnight?

then I understand

The sweet dark liquid
tastes like life.

Ziinzibaakwadwaaboo

Apii gooniwaabooyaan giiskamaan,
apii aandegwag niimiwaad anaamayi'iing mitigoog
apii e-odishiwejig dagoshinowaad noopimiing
miidash ziinzibaakwadwaaboo bagidinamaan
zhiwagamizigan bazhidebii
ziibiin ziigwang bazhidebii.

Shkaakaamikwe dagoshino agwajiing
zaagiaad miinawaa zaagiaawaad
mikawaamaad gakina gashiwag
aawiwaad daanisag apane igo.

Sweet Water

When the blanket of snow is removed
when crows dance beneath the trees
when visitors arrive among the branches
I offer them sweet water
the sap of their dreams
rivers of spring overflowing.

The weather a mother made new
who loves as she is loved
reminds every mother
she is always a daughter.

Jiijak

I'widi anaamidibikigiizis
besho waasamitig
agiji'aazhibikong
gagiibaadaanagidoon jiijak gaabawid.
Mikwenimaa ina? Mikwendaan ina?
Manidoonsag ina gi gii maawaag?
Miinikaanan ina gi gii miijinaanan?

Gaawiin gego ni gii noondoosiinoon
besho metaa'asiniinsag
anong-awanibiisaa
mii gaaskanazoyaan.
Aaniin ezhiwebag agwajiing i'widi?
Aaniin ezhiwebag biinjayiing gdo'ode?

Crane

Under the night sun
near the far tree
atop the stone cliff
the crazy crane is standing.
Remembering who? Remembering what?
Insects eaten? Seeds that satisfied?

I hear nothing
in the star mist
far from the worn pebbles
so I whisper.
How's the weather over there?
Are storms or sunshine in your heart?

Niigaanianimosh

Megwaa giiweyaan animosh gii nagishkawaa.

Ozhinaagwi'aan oma'iinganan.

Maamakaadizi apii gii ni dagoshinoyaan.

Miidash nangaaj wiidosemidizoyaang

    indigo wiiji-ayaadiyaang chizhaazhi gwa

        niizh kaadan . . . niiwin kaadan . . . ingodwaaswi

    getin neseyaang noodinong

        biinjaya'ii . . . agwajiing . . . giiwitaa'aya'ii

    ozidan miikanong bima'adoyaang

        maamwi gikendamaang e-bangishimod

    baabinchiged . . . biidaaban waabang.

The Lead Dog

On the way home I met a dog.

He had the look of a lean but satisfied wolf.

He was curious when I arrived.

Then slowly we matched steps

    as if we had been together long ago

              two legs . . . four legs . . . six

    panting the same wind

            in . . . out . . . around

    feet following the same path

            knowing together the sun isn't setting

    it is waiting for us . . . on the other dayside.

Waasnoode

Naanan awesiiyag gii maamwi-babaamaadiziwag
megwa Nokomis-nibaa-giiizis gii giizhigong inikodang.

Mizizaakoons gii gawajise,
"Giizhigong ozhaawaashkong dibishkoo nd'oshkiinzhigoong."

Waabooz gii ninangibizo,
"Giizhigong baswewe onitawageng."

"Ni wii niim"gaaskanazod ginebeg,
"dibishkoo zenibaanh aazhawayi'iing zhingwaakwag."

"Giiwedin jaaginazhishin"
gii gaaskanazod omakakii.

Megwaa gii enendamo animosh,
"Niminaandawaag, giizhigong-giosejig."

Northern Lights

Five animals traveled together
while grandmother moon sliced the sky.

Deerfly zummed,
"The sky is as green as my eyes."

Rabbit trembled,
"The sky echoes in my ears."

"I will dance," whispered Snake
"like a ribbon behind the pines."

"I want this wind to consume me,"
whispered the frog.

Meanwhile, dog thought,
"I smell the sky-hunters."

Waasa Waabaamaa

Waasawad mikwamizhingwaakwaandagoog,

   beshowad waagitawagan

      wanishkweyendamigad

         bidaasige miinawaa

            wiisagendamowin minjimendamaan.

Concerning Distance

As far away as frozen pine tips

    as close as ears curved

        is the distraction

           of a sunrise and

               a pain remembered.

Aa . . .

Aabitaa-dibikad apii

Aabaabiigindizoying

Aazhigijishinoying

Aawendamang

Aanzinaagodizoyang.

Ah . . .

At midnight

We unwind

We fall back

And recognize

Our revolution.

Naanoogizhkaa

Nimanidoowaabikoow.
Giwiikobizhin.
Mii giwiikobidaw
 maamakaajichigeyin
 awan didibinamaang
 awi dibiki-giizis
 miinawaa baagishid
 naawi-aki.
Gigoozomin.
Ginagwaazhidizomin.
Gidagoodemin
 giizhigong.

Inertia

I am magnetic.
I move you.
I make you pull
    until you miraculously
    break my inertia
    water rolling
    toward the moon
    earth swelling
    from the center.
We balance.
We snare.
We hang
    in heaven's heat.

Maamwi Aabitoose

Inini ni dagooshino.

Ikwen da iskapozhaan ina gii gagwejimdizod.
   "Nimbiingej" gii ikido, "aabitojishin."

Miidash epiichi gaaskwe giizhig
   gii ziiginang jichaakwaaboo.

Maamwi-okaadendizowag . . .
oninjiin akeyaa giiwedinong miinawaa dibikanong
oninjiin akeyaa zhaawanong miinawaa waabanong
kaadenigewaad dibishkoo ojiibikan maage aanakwad-jiibikan.

Maamwi aabitoose giizhigong miinawaa aakiing . . .
waabmaangidwa Giizis, Dibikigiizis, miinawaa gakina Gete-jiibayag
nesewaad gaawiin enendamosiiwaad
boochiwewaad gaawiin ikidosiiwaad.

Aabitoose,

   aabitoose,

      aabitoose,

         aabitoose.

Together Between

The man arrives.

He thinks of drinking the woman.
   "I'm cold," he says, "hold me."

And then while the sky hums
   she pours the liquid of her soul.

Together they are braided . . .
fingers in the direction of the evening star
fingers in the direction of the morning star
woven like roots or cloud stems.

Together between heaven and earth . . .
they are seen by the Sun, the Moon, and the Old Ghosts
they breathe without thinking
they converse without speaking.

Mixed,

   in the center,

      one half,

         the other half.

Ganawenimidizowag

Weweni ganawenimidizowag
ozhaawashkoziwag giiwitaabizonikewaad
mitigwakiing.

Weweni gegaa boodawadizowag
anami-kchizhaawashkowaaseyaagiizhigong
waabaandamowaad zhibaasige
nisodotamowaad wenji-gizhimaadziyaang.

Careful

Careful, aware of one another
they form a green circle
in the woods.

Careful, nearly on fire
beneath blue-bright heavens
they see the clearing sky
and understand the power of heat.

Giizis Gizhookawaan

Bezhig be bezhig obizhishigonaan.
Bezhig be bezhig waa obazhidebazhaan,
   giizis gizhookawaan
   nese shkizoongi'aan
   ziigaashi'aan gaashwan.
Dooskaabiwag,
daawaniwag,
baakaakonama'aa dibikong, biidaaban.

Warmed by the Sun

One by one they are emptied.
One by one they will be overflowing,
    made warm by the sun
    breath materialized
    poured by maternity.
Eyes opening,
eyes closing,
they are exalted in the night, in the dawn.

Gabe-agindaaso

Niizhiwag, biimiskobizowaad
gizhibaawaashiwaad
didibaabizowaad, giizhigo-maadagewaad
Giizis, Dibiki-giizis, ganjiwebinidizowaad.

Gabe-agindaaso.

Agwaayaashkaa,
animaashkaa,
ezhi-dakobinaaying
ezhi-daaskaaying.

Eternal Counting

As a pair, they rotate
turning in the wind,
spinning, swimming in the sky
Sun, Moon, pushing one another.

Eternal counting.

The tide comes in,
the tide goes out,
the way we are all bound,
the way we all unravel.

Daanisag

Apane gidaanikooshininim dibishkoo
nigiig niizhoninjiiniwaad
megwaa agwanjinwaad
enji-agwaamowaad gemaa enji-nibaawaad.

Miskweyaabiin gi gii maada'oonidimin
mii noongom ezhi-bimaadiziying
bizwaabiigisin miinawaa basangwaabiying
agwaabijigeying, boonakanjigeying.

Apii jagazigaade giizhigad
ishkode-bingwinan zhaabosaamang
zhingob-miinan wii mikamang
miinawaa misko-miin-ojiibikan.

Gi ga gikinoo'amawininim
ezhi-noondawangidwa maanidoog
ezhi-biizikamang waasnoode
ezhi-aanzinaagodizoying dibikong

ezhi-dabasendamoying boochigo dibishkoo
                    bezhig
    manidoominens   *giizis*   agogwaazod
                bakaanizid.

Daughters

Our connection is like
otters holding hands
floating together
on the sea and in sleep.

Once shared veins
became a way of life
tangled and blinking
casting nets and anchors.

And when your days burn down
I will sift ashes with you
to find the pine seeds
and raspberry roots.

I will teach you
to hear the spirits shake
to wear the northern lights
to shift shapes in the night

to believe in the beautiful humility
           of one
bead   *sun*   sewn
        differently.

E-nookaaznamowaad

Omisenyan miinawaa oshiimeyan nookaaznaamowaad:
    Ogashewaa ginoo-giizhigoon
    Oswaa nibe-dibikadoon
    Waazakonenjiganaa-waabandizowinan
    Gakina inaandeg gimiwang
    Ikidowinan eta ndo'mazina'igananing
    Abita eta ezhi-nimiiyaan
    Mii odewaa nagamowaad.

What They Use

The sisters use:
    Their mother's long days
    Their father's sleepy nights
    Mirrors with lights
    All the colors of the rain
    From my books, the words only
    From my dance, every other step
    From their hearts, their own songs

Gimiizhaanaanig

Miigwanag gimiizhaanaanig,
miisanajiiwayaanag biizikamowaad
epiichii dibishkoo minojiwan ezhi-nimiiwaad.

Miidash ozaawigwanewag
wiisaakodeg wiisaakodeng
aabitaa mitigomizh, aabitaa ginebigobag.

Mizaatigan
anaaganashk aawiwaad
adaawejig enji-nawanj-adaawewin.

Giniijaanisinaanig wawezhi'aangwaa
ashamangwaa oshki-enendamowinan
mii ganbaj gaawiin waa miigaadisiiwaad.

We Give Them

We give them plumes and quills,
and downy tips to wear
while dancing like smooth currents.

They become golden-feathered
half-breeds in the burnt forest
part oak, part fern.

Solid branches,
soft bracken, they are
traders in an evolved economy.

Our decorated children
nourished on new ideas
possibly able to avoid old battlefields.

Miskwiyiwigiizhig Gichigamigong

Miskwiyiwigiizhigong ezhi-bangishimo

epaaskaakonizhibiiaanang

biidaashkaang

jiimaaning jiimsawensan

biimskojiwan gichigamigong

awaazisii asiniiwan

gaaskachigamotawaad

ayaawaad namwaanzhibiing.

Red Sky over Superior

At sunset in the lowering

brilliance is written

on the arriving tide

where kisses are ships

curved against the sea

and a clan fish whispers

the language of waves

to the stones of a subterranean cave.

Giizis miinawaa Dibikigiizis

Giizis, dibikgiizis miinawaa
waasaa wiikweyaa gidaaw.

Makademitigomiizhonegek miinawaa
ojiishiwiigwaas gidaaw.

Getemiikanan oodenang, waawaashkeshbimikawewinan
miinawaa ezhi-ipogozi namepin gikendaman.

Mikwenminaan, weneniminaan
aagawaateshining giizhigong, dibikong.

Sun and Moon

You are the sun and the moon
and the sky-bright bay to me.

You are the crevices of black oak
and scarred shine of white birch.

You know cobbled roads and deer paths
and the taste of wild ginger.

You are all I know and all I forget
in the shadow of day and the arc of night.

Nimaaminonendaan

Gaawiin nigiizhiitaasii.
Gaawiin zegizisiiyaan.
Nigikenmaag Nimkiig
Giiwitaabizowag indeng
miskwa-ziibii
gizho-bawating.
Okaanag aangodinong
aawiwag wesiinhyag.
Apane apii maaminonendamoyaan
maamakaadenidizoyaan.

I Realize

This is no conclusion.
I am not afraid.
I know the Thunderbirds.
They swirl around my heart
a red river
of fiery rapids.
Sometimes the tame
are once again wild.
And always realizations
are astonishing.

Aangodinong

Waawoono ma'iingan apii owaabamaan oshkagoojin.
Waawaasiso epiichi nagamod dibikong.
Ishpaa'ii waaskone-aazhogan zhamaaganish aawid.
Onaanaagadawaabamaan oshkimanidoowan
dagooshinowaad omisad nameg anaamibiig.
Aangodinong ma'iingan nindaaw apii nagamoyaan,
aangodingong name nindaaw apii anaami'aayaan,
aaba'amaan miigaadiwin.

Sometimes

The wolf howls at the new moon.
He sparkles while he sings in the night.
He's an overpass light brigade soldier.
He carefully watches the new spirits
arriving in the belly of the sturgeon below.
Sometimes I am a wolf singing,
sometimes I am a sturgeon praying,
on the way to un-make war.

Anokiiwin

Bebezhig aniibiishag
baakisewag giizisong.

Bebeshing ojiibikag
zhiibaawaanikewag.

Nindanokii ji-nisidotamaan
ndojichaagan

miidash maaminonendamaan
bimaadiziwin miinawaa ezhi-minobimaadizi.

---

*Aniibiishan miinawaa ojiibikan omaa ni gii aanjitoonan mii aabijiibaawaad.

Work

The work of every leaf
is to open in the sun.

The work of every root
is to tunnel through the earth.

My work is to recognize
the interior of my soul

and wonder at the difference
between life and living.

---

*Leaves and roots, which are often spoken of as inanimate
in Anishinaabemowin, are changed to come alive in this poem.*

Noongom miinawaa awaswaabang, booch nisidotawdizoyang gaye nisidot-
angidwa mayagizijig, manaadenimangwaa miinawaa maamakaadiziyang
ezhi-bimaadiziyang.

Emma Goldman, 1906

Nakweshkodaadidaa

Mewinzha
dagonigaademigad
gii goshkwaakobizhinang
ondaadiziyang giizhigong
miinawaa akiing.

Noongom zhaabwiiyang
goshkwaawaadiziyang
nisidotawdizoying
mashkomikwendamang
gakina awiiyaa inawendiyang.

Nakweshkodaadidaa
noongom aakiing omaa
jibwaa jiibayag aayaaying
biizikamang naabikawaagan anangag
waabamangwaa giniijaanisnaanig.

The problem that confronts us today, and which the nearest future is to solve, is how to be oneself, and yet in oneness with others, to feel deeply with all human beings and still retain one's own characteristic qualities.

Emma Goldman, 1906

The Way We Meet

Long ago in the mixing
we were shaken
in every direction
different children
of the sky and the land.

To survive now we must
be at peace in our hearts
understand one another
and bravely remember
we are all, one by one, cousins.

Let's meet one another
here now on earth before
we become heavenly ancestors
wearing a necklace of stars
visible to our heirs.

Bíonn dúil le béal farraige ach cha bhíonn dúil le béal uaighe.
Gichigamigong gimbagosendaamin. Jiibegamigong gaawiin
gimbanaadendansiimin.

Ulster proverb

Gichigaming Oniijaanisag Onjibaawag

Gichigaming ningashki bagosendaamyaan
jiibegamigong anami'aayaan nazhikewiziyaan.

Aaniin waa inakamigad apii baasigaade okanan,
apii aniibiishan izhinaagwad mitigoonsan,
apii zhiiwitaagani-gokoshitawagan?

Maamawimaajaamigad ina
Anishinaabemowin
miinawaa nesewin?

Enya . . . gemaa . . . wanitooyangoba
apii gaawiin noondansiiwang gichigaming
miinawaa waamdamang bizhishigwaag jiibegamigan.

Bíonn dúil le béal farraige ach cha bhíonn dúil le béal uaighe.
There is hope from the mouth of the sea but not from the
mouth of the grave.

Ulster proverb

Children of the Waters

In the sea I can hope
in the grave I pray alone.

What happens when the bones are dried,
when the little leaves have become sticks,
when the sow's ears are in salt?

Do they leave together
the language and
the last breath?

Yes . . . maybe yes . . . it will be lost
when we no longer hear the open waters
and we see our graves are empty.

Ogiiaande

Ninaagadawenimaa Amelian

Dibaajimotawishin oginii-moshwe.

Nitaam, adoopowiniigan gii gidaaw
miidash gegoo gii daapnamaan ji-mikwenimag
Miigwechwigiizhigong ezhi-jiibaakwed.

Noongom gimbiizikawaag
waabizenibaag miinawaa
niimikawinaan
niimikawagwaa nidaanisag
niimikawagwaa okomisag
gii zisinaaganewaad Miigwechwigiizhigong.

Anishinaabeikwewag
gizhibashimowaad
ji-minobimaadiziwaad
ji-ganawendizowaad
ji-bamenimaawaad oniijaanisag
e-anami-gashkibijigankejig
miinawaa oginiimaadiziwaad.

Pink

For Amelia

Talk to me, pink shawl.

First, you were a tablecloth
then you were something I took
to remember her Thanksgiving.

Now you wear
white ribbons and I dance
for you
for my daughters
for all the grandmothers
who set tables of thanksgiving.

Anishinaabe women
round dance together
to live well
to care for each another
to care for the children
who make bundles
of prayer and pink life.

Waawiyebii'igeyaang

Ningiizhibii'amawaa Daphne Odjig

Maajaamigad maage maajitaamigad
apii dibaajimoyang?
Nindoninaaminan ina ikidowinan dibishkoo
nimishoomisinaanig miinwa nookomisinaanig?

Ningashki'oomin ina gikenimangidwa
aanzheniig oziigiziwaad wiigwaasing,
zakide waabigwaniin,
gichitwaadewegewinan?

Ningashki'oomin ina waabmangidwa
jiibayag niimiwaad
dibishkoo baapaaseg
bakadewaad miinawaa baapaagaakwa'igewaad?

Giisphin biindigawiyaang oshki-akiing.
wii debisiniiyaang, miigisag bingweng
wii aawiyaang migiziyag agijiaatig,
jingwaanan giizhigong.

Maajaayaang apane
maajitaayaang apane
dibaajimoyaang apane
waawiyebii'igeyaang.

Circle Images

For Daphne Odjig

Is it leaving or is it beginning
the way we tell stories?
Do we assemble words like
our grandfathers and our grandmothers?

Can we know them
as wrinkled birchbark angels
flowers on fire
or firm honor beats?

Can we see their
spirits dancing
like woodpeckers
hungry and knocking?

If we enter new worlds
we will be satisfied shells in the sand
eagles tipping treetops
meteors in the sky.

We are always beginning
we are always leaving
we are always storying
writing circles.

Megwaa aadizookaanag inenimangidwaa, ozhibii'iganan, ikidowinan, nametoowinan apiichi gagwedwemigad mii bangii eta nakomigaade. Giisphin Aadizookaanag naagadawenimangidwaa, ganabaj gaawiin ashiwiisiiyang ji-nisidotamaang—ezhi-bimaadiziyaang, ezhi-inendaagoziyaang, ezhi-inaakonigeyaang, ezhi-adaaweyang, ezhi-jaaginigeyaang. Bezhig bimaadizid gaawiin owaabandansiin gakina akeyaa, ganabaj giiwedin gemaa zhaawanong gemaa ishpiming miinawaa anaaming. Ganabaj apii aadizookaanag inenimangwaa gegaa waabandamang gakina akeyaa.

Gordon Henry

Ode'ng

Ningoogii
ode'ng
okong
omisadong
aanjitooyaan
ningaabaaweyaan
    zhaab-odoodikwasiwagong
                zhaab-onagazhiining
agindamaan e-gikendamaan miskweyaabiing
giziibiiga'amaan wenda-debwemigad.
Okaninawemaagan aawiyang.
Aabita eta gikedamang nisawayii neseyang.

As we work in Native Literature, we find that most terms, most linguistic signs, signals and attachments raise as many questions as they answer. If we go deeper we may end up in areas of cognitive reorientation that demand we engage the world in ways that our field may not yet be prepared to undertake—for social, political, economic, psychological, historically and culturally rationalized reasons, among other things. No one person holds 100% of indigenous cultural competencies we might associate with world-view (Anishinaabeg knowledge), maybe someone in this space or place has 5%, maybe someone else holds 25%, maybe, through some kind of collective knowledge we draw closer to that 100%.

Gordon Henry

Into a Heart

I am diving
into a heart
a liver
a stomach
changing
dissolving
through kidneys
       through intestines
counting what I know in my veins
washing all of what it true.
We are bone relatives.
Each knowing half
between breaths.

Aloha - Aaniin

Naaway'ii aki miinawaa gichigaming
gaawiin aawasiin gegoo
gemaa gakina gego aawan.

Jiimaanan gii bagami-ayaamagad
megwaa aanind nibaawaad
miinawaa aanind nibowaad.

Papa miinawaa Wakea oganawaabamaawaan
miinawaa aanind bakinagewaad,
aanind banaadenjigewaad

Gigikinawaabamin ina
ezhi-gondamaang
ningaabikwaaboo?

Gigikinawaabamin ina
ezhi-agonamaang
mamaangaashkaa?

---

*Aloha *miinawaa* aniin *ikidoyaang anamikodaading gaye* aloha *ikidoyaang*
enji-zaagiding gaye aaniin *enji-gagweding.*

Aloha - Aaniin

Between the land and the sea
there is nothing
or there is everything.

Boats arrive
as some are sleeping
and some are dying.

Papa and Wakea watch
as some are winning
and others lose hope.

Can we ever learn
to swallow
lava?

Can we ever learn
to hold
the waves?

---

*Aloha *and* aniin *are used as greetings.* Aloha *is also part of many phrases related to* love while *aaniin* has a second meaning which relates to continual questioning.*

Dine Aki

Nimikwenimaag ikwewag gii niibawiwaad basaabikaang
                                        —*Verna, Debbie, Gloria, and Carolyn*

Gakina gegoo Dine akiing
    okosimaanaande
    waasaamiskwaasiin
    ishkwaabiisaa

    giisawaande
    megwaa ikwewag
    nandomaawaad maanishtaanishag

    makwa'aande
    megwaa ininiwag
    nibaawaad anaami'anangoog.

Gaawiin bakaansadsiinoon
    apii anami'aayang waabanong
    gdo'*hogan* izhinaagwad wiigiwaam

    apii aaniin kidoyaan
    izhinaataagwad *aahhnee*

    apii *beesh* ikidoyan
    izhinaataagwad biizh.

Gaganoonidiying, nagamoying
miinawaa gichimiigwechiwenimangwaa
Haashch'ééh miinawaa Gichimanidoo naasaab.

Ikidowinan:
hogan = wiigiwam
aahhnee = miigwech
beesh = aaniin
Haashch'ééh = Niiwin gichimanidoog

74

Dine Land

For the women who stand at the edge of the canyon
—Verna, Debbie, Gloria, and Carolyn

Everything in Dine country is
    pumpkin-pink
    red rock shining
    after the rain

    sun-colored
    while the women
    call to their sheep

    bear-colored
    while the men
    sleep under the stars.

It is not so different at all
    when we pray to the east
    in your *hogan* shaped like a *wigwam.*

    when I say aaniin
    it sounds like aahhnee

    when you say *beesh*
    it sounds like *biizh.*

We visit and sing
and give the same thanks
to Haashch'ééh and Gichimanidoo,

Words:
hogan = wigwam = round house
aahhnee = thanks
aaniin = beesh = hello
Haashch'ééh = Four Dine Holy People

Ziigwang, Argentinajig miinidiwag miinawaa mazina'iganan atoowaad
ingojiing bimaadizid ji-mikang. Mii wi ezhinikaade "suelta de libros."
Guaranijig onjibawag besho Perito Moreno Mikwami-wajiw.

Aabita Waasa

Aazhawe-akiing, besho mikwamii-wajiw. apii maajii-ziigwang.
Zaaga'jigaabawiwaad zaagijig, waabigwanan aawiwaad
atoowaad zaagibii'anan agwajiing
gitigaan-apabiwining, chi-odaabaaning, mitigong.

Aazhawe-akiing, besho Gichigaming, apii maajii-dagwaaging.
Dibaajimojig miinawaa waanikejig
anaami-giiyose-giizis wiikondiwaad
boodawewewaad ji-baabiitoowaad baboon.

In spring in Argentina, people celebrate "suelta de libros" by leaving books in public for others to find. It is also the place of the Guarani people and the world's largest glacier, Perito Moreno.

Halfway Away

On one side of the earth, near the ice-mountain, Spring begins.
Lovers step out, open as flowers
to leave sonnets, odes, and verse
on benches, on busses, and branches.

On another side of the earth, near the Great Sea, Fall begins.
Storytellers and cache-diggers
feast under the hunting moon
and light fires to wait for winter.

Dagoshinowag

Oshki giizis miinawaa oshki biboon maajtaamigad.
Jiibay-miikan waawaasaabikide giizhigong
geyabi e-nibojig gashkaabika'igaazowaad.

Agwajing gisinaasige gaye bagamaanimad.
Ishpaagonagaa Zhingwaak biizikang ziibaaska'iganan
miinawaa biidwewese megwa ondamitaayaang odeng.

Zhiingenjigejig, meyagazidjig miinawaa wiiji'odoodemijig
da mikwendamowaad ensa okan
da mikwenimaawaad ensa ojichaag.

Noondawangwa biinish bagidenimangwa
zhigajiii'owaad Jiibinaakewin . . .

*Anishinaabe-Jiibaygamig-Giiweodoonan (NAGPRA) gii nakinigewin 1990, gaye
maashi bagidinigaazsiiwag.*

They Arrive

A new month and new year have arrived.
The Road of Ghosts is blue in the heavens
and still the ones who left are prisoners.

Outdoors, cold sunshine greets a hard wind.
In the deep snow, pine wears ice jingles
heard by our busy hearts.

Enemies, strangers, and clan relatives
should remember every bone
should remember every soul.

We can hear them and until they are released
they tire waiting for the next Feast of the Dead . . .

Though the Native American Graves Protection and Repatriation Act was decided in 1990, not all remains have been reburied.

Waawaatesiwag

Aaniin ezhi-pogozid dibikigiizis?

Aaniin ezhi-pogwad waasamowin?
Aaniin ezhichigeyaamba
ji-nisidostawaag waawaatesiwag?
Nimbagamaashi ina giizhigong
gemaa bimaakogomoyaan ode'agaming?

Waa ninzaka'amawdiz ganabaj
atooyaan ishkodensan ishpiming
anangziibikeyaan dibikong
miidash bizaani-ayaayaan
dibishkoo baashkaabigwan-ininiwizh.

Fireflies

How does one taste the moon?

What is the weight of wind?
How can I understand
the fireflies?
Sail kisses to heaven
or row to a heart's shore?

Perhaps I will set myself alight
place the flames in the sky
make a night river of light
then become as quiet as
a milkweed blossom.

Wazhashkoog Wazhashkwedoonsing

Enji-bagone'ong gaajigaazowag

akakanzhe'aanzowag ojichaagensag

Anishinaabemaazowaad . . .

"Okanwaan ginikanminaanig

gaye ojiibikan gibozowaad

megwa minikweyangmashkiigwaaboo

ziinzibaakwadwaabo gii wanendameg

mii bagidendaagoziyaang

ji-niimiyaang wazhashkwedoonsing."

Muskrats in Mushrooms

In the hole where they hide

their little grey souls

they sing in Anishinaabemowin . . .

"Our cousins' bones

with the roots are roasting

while we drink the swamp water

syrup you have all forgotten

so we are free

dancing in the mushrooms."

Negaaj Igo

Nin gii babaamosemin megwaayaak
    negaaj igo . . . negaaj igo
mii ni dagoshinoyang mitaawangaa gii aanjinaanakwad
    negaaj igo . . . negaaj igo
megwaa gaganoonidiyang, gdo'ikidowinan gii asiginmaan
    negaaj igo . . . negaaj igo
mashkawmashkiki ishkomaan inde'ng
    negaaj igo . . . negaaj igo
asiniig babaamiweba'ogowaad enji-jiimiding
    negaaj igo . . . negaaj igo.

Gaawiin bimosesiiyaang mashkiiganing
    wenji nookaa
    mii sa zhingishiniyang
    negaaj igo . . . negaaj igo.

Slowly

We walked through the woods
    slowly . . . slowly
to arrive at the beach as the clouds were changing
    slowly . . . slowly
there, while we visited, I gathered your words
    slowly . . . slowly
they are strong medicine I save in my heart
    slowly . . . slowly
they are rocks washed ashore by water's kiss
    slowly . . . slowly.

We cannot walk in this swamp
    because it is too soft
    so we lie down
    slowly . . . slowly.

Nitaa-niigaaniin

Niigaaniin ezhi-mookodaman mikwam,

zhiiwitaamiskwi zhaabose.

Nisidotan gwiinawaabanjigaade gaye

gaawiin gashki'osiiyan aaba'igeyan.

Gikendan anaamiindim anjisemigad

ningoding aagawaatewin aawid giigoonh.

Fundamentals of Leadership

Like ice carving lakes on continents,

like blood salt passing through cells.

Understand what is unseen

and what cannot be undone.

Know in the depths of change

sometimes the shadows are fish.

Jiibay Minjimendaagozi

Jiibay midewaatig ogii azhegandinan
naasaab gii tood mewinzha dibikad
apii Wenona wiindamawaad Ningaabii'aninoodin,
"Awashme gizaagin waasa aayaayin."

Gekek-dip ogii gwekinan,
ishkwaandem inaasamisin
mimigowebidood gaanda'igwaasonan
daanginaad manidoominensag.

Mii minjimenimaad
maamakaadenimowaad
waawaatesi-shkiinzhiwewag
naanaagadawaabaamaawaad.

Wenona miinawaa Ningaabii'aninoodin
webinaad, boonigidetaadiwaad
minjimendad gaa inakamigad
jibwaa jiibay aawid.

The Ghost Remembers

The ghost moved the ceremonial stick
back to where it was that long-ago night
when Wenona told the West Wind
"I love you more when you are away."

The ghost turned the hawk's head
to face the door,
shook the thimbles
touched the beads.

And remembered them all
amazed
eyes lit like fireflies
watching.

Wenona and the West Wind
separating, forgiving
remembering the past
before she became the ghost.

Bagidenim

Ningii manidoowigashkibijiganke
gashkibizhagwaa maakadewaasiniig
bagidenimadiz mii gashkitooyaan
bagidenimagwaa gakina asiniig gii aayaawaad
anaamibiig megwa anokiiyaan
anaamaatig megwa nitaawigiyaan
anaamaawang dagonigaade zhiiwitaagan
anaamaagon bi gii ningizoyaan
noojimod nindojichaag
gashkibjigankeyaan.

To Forgive

I made a spirit bundle
wrapped the black stones
and forgave myself so I could
forgive all the ones who were
below the water while I worked
below the woods where I grew
below the sands mixed with salt
under the snow where I dissolved
healing my spirit
making a bundle.

Mooka'am Giizis

Gaawiin wiikaa giizis mooka'amsii.
Giboozinodaanaan eta akiing
besho mashkwizid
miidash washkigiiweyang.

Gaawiin wiikaa gigikinoo'amawaasiinaanig.
Gidibaajimotawaanaanig eta
gigizheb biinish onaagoshin,
niibin binish biboon.

Gaawiin nimbookochishkaasiimin.
Nindapangishimin biidaashkaang
aaswaakogaabawiyaang
gaawiin waabandansiiwaang aanjibimaadiziyaang.

Rising Sun

The sun never really rises.
We only ride earth toward
that force and energy
and then rotate away.

We never really teach.
We tell measured stories
morning to afternoon
summer to winter.

We never really break.
We fall back in the crashing waves
to stand up once again
not seeing how we've changed.

Gaawiin Nizhaagooji'igoosiig

Apii debwewin ninandawaabandaan
Binji-waanzhing, anaami-jiibayag niimi'idiwag
gakina manidoog miigwechiwiaagwaa
gii waabamid babaamiseyaan dibikong.

Miidash ninisidotawaa nindojichaak
awashime ninode gikendamaan
ezhi-gaa-dibajimowaad gichi-aya'aag
ezhi-waa-bimaadizowaad oniijaanisag.

I Am Undefeated

While searching for the truth
in caves and under the Northern lights
I thank all the spirits
for seeing my flight at night.

And perhaps my soul understands
more than my heart can know
about the knowledge of elders
and the possibile lives of children.

Acknowledgments

Nimiigwechwiaag, many thanks, to the editors of the following publications in which some of these poems appeared in sometimes translated and slightly altered versions:

Verse Wisconsin
"Waawoono / Howling" and
"Mii Miigwanag Miizhangidwaa / What We Gave Them"

Cream City Review
"We Are Returning Always"

Contemporary Native American Poets
"Michigan to Argentina" and "Together Between"

Harper's Ferry Review
"Dinebikeyah" and "Waagaamitigoog"

Yukhika Latuhse / She Tells Us Stories: A Journal of the Oneida Nation Arts Program
"Dine Land (Dinebikayah)"

Voice On the Water: Great Lakes Native America Now
"Kaanan / Bones," "Wazhashwag Wazhashkwedong / Muskrats in Mushrooms," and "Manoomin / Wild Rice"

Michigan Quarterly Review
"Waawaateseg / Fireflies" and "N'gii Zhibiiamaag Niijaanisag Chigamigong / A Poem for the Children of the Great Lakes"

Sing: Poetry from the Indigenous Americas
"Dibikiziigwaagaame: Night Syrup"

Water Stone Review
"Geyabi Ingoding Manido-Giizisong / Once Again In January"

Yellow Medicine Review
"Nengatch Gwa"

Miinawaa miigwechwiagwaa giizis, dibikigiizis, akiing miinawaa gichigaming miinawa gakina nisawayi'ii aayaawaad. It is hard to single out specific individuals when clearly the moon, the sun, the earth, and great lakes have given the gift of inspiration. I am indebted to all my family who have supported my wordplay through the years and the friends and fellow poets who continue to encourage me.